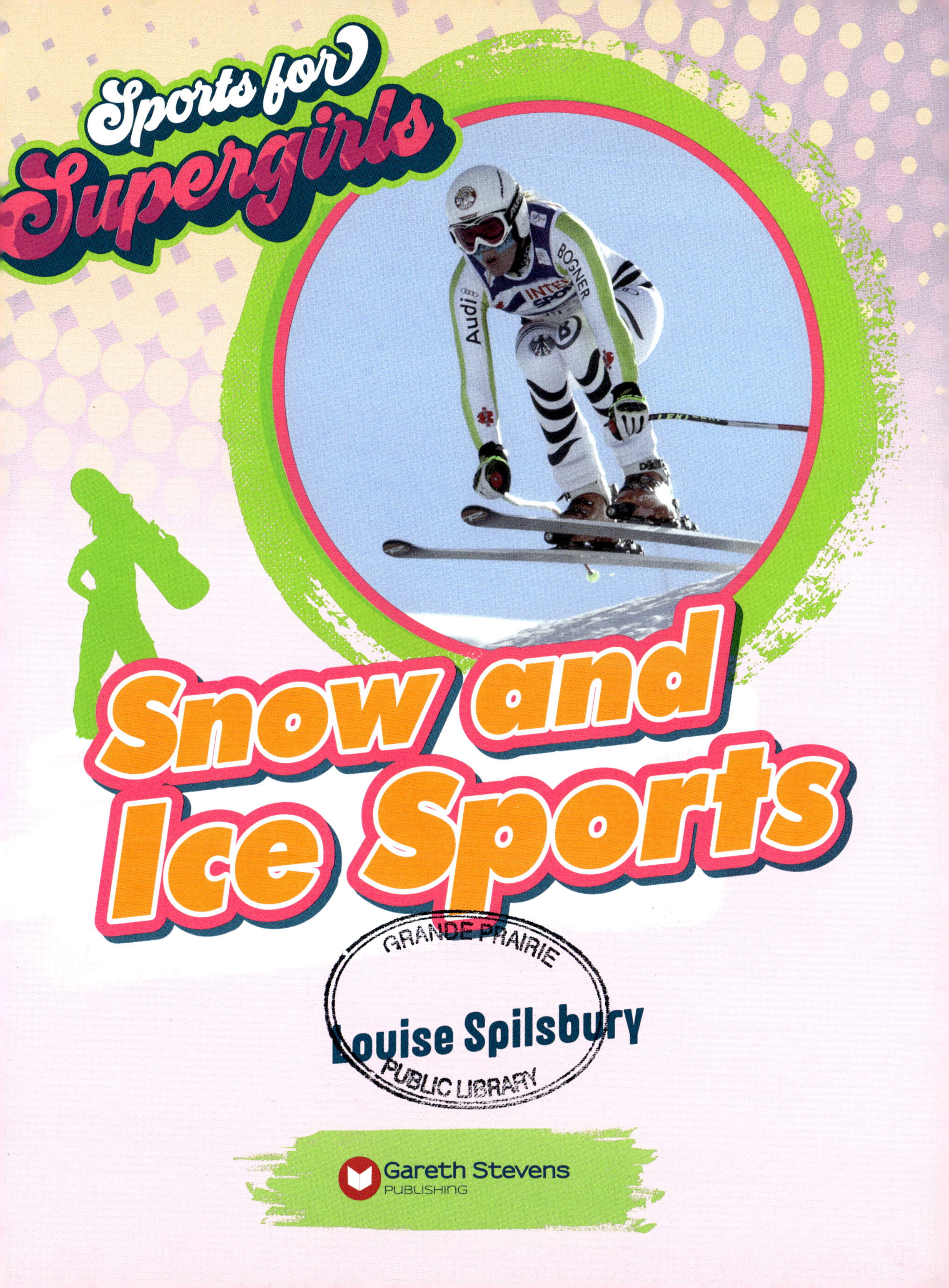

Sports for Supergirls

Snow and Ice Sports

Louise Spilsbury

Gareth Stevens
PUBLISHING

Please visit our website, **www.garethstevens.com**.
For a free color catalog of all our high-quality books,
call toll free 1-800-542-2595 or fax 1-877-542-2596.

Cataloging-in-Publication Data

Names: Spilsbury, Louise.
Title: Snow and ice sports / Louise Spilsbury.
Description: New York : Gareth Stevens Publishing, 2020. | Series: Sports for supergirls | Includes glossary and index.
Identifiers: ISBN 9781538242186 (pbk.) | ISBN 9781538241912 (library bound)
Subjects: LCSH: Winter sports--Juvenile literature. | Women athletes--Juvenile literature.
Classification: LCC GV841.15 S65 2020 | DDC 796.9--dc23

First Edition

Published in 2020 by
Gareth Stevens Publishing
111 East 14th Street, Suite 349
New York, NY 10003

Produced by Calcium
Editors: Sarah Eason and Jennifer Sanderson
Designers: Clare Webber, Jeni Child, and Jessica Moon

Photo credits: Cover: Shutterstock: YanLev; Inside: Shutterstock: 4Max: p. 43t; Kuznetsov Alexey: p. 32; Close Encounters Photo: p. 17t; Corepics VOF: p. 25; eWilding: p. 31; Mitch Gunn: pp. 1, 6; Herrndorff: p. 17b; Stefan Holm: pp. 7, 8; Olha Insight: p. 9t; Goran Jakus: pp. 9b, 45; Gornostay: p. 30; Jeannette Meier Kamer: p. 4; Alexey Kartsev : p. 22; Kubais : p. 19t; Lucky Business : p. 16; Marek CECH: p. 28; Sergey Mironov: p. 43b; Vitalii Nesterchuk: p. 29; Iurii Osadchi: pp. 5, 23b; PhotoStock10: p. 10; Sportpoint: p. 24; StockphotoVideo: p. 26; Yulia_B: p. 19b; Vadim Zakharishchev: p. 18; Leonard Zhukovsky: pp. 20, 21t. 21b, 27; Kendra Stritch: p. 33; Wikimedia Commons: 121a0012: pp. 38, 38, 40, 41; Ailura: pp. 1, 12, 15; Sandro Halank: pp. 3, 34, 35t, 35b, 36-37, 37; Korea.net (http://www.korea.net) / Korean Culture and Information Service (Korean Olympic Committee): p. 42; Manuguf : p. 14; MartinPutz : p. 13b; Reywas92: p. 13t; VateGV: p. 23t.

CPSIA compliance information: Batch #CS19GS:
For further information contact Gareth Stevens, New York, New York at 1-800-542-2595.

Contents

Chapter 1

Carving Their Own Path

Snow and ice sports can be daring and dangerous, which is perhaps why, in the past, they were mostly enjoyed by men. But not anymore! Today, women are strapping on their skis and riding on their snowboards to show the world that they can carve their own paths through the powder in these exciting sports.

Skiers love the excitement and drama of speeding down a slope covered in snow, sending up a wave of powder as they turn!

WHAT ARE SNOW AND ICE SPORTS?

Snow and ice sports, as their name suggests, are any sports that take place on snow or iced surfaces. They include skiing, ski jumping, snowboarding, sledding, ice-skating, hockey, and more. They require fitness and strength, which is another reason why they may have been thought of as male-only territory, but girls and women are blowing the lid off that outdated idea in a big way. They are flocking to the snowy slopes and ice rinks to get fit, have fun, and compete in front of large, enthusiastic crowds.

IN OR OUT?

Snow and ice sports are not only for those who live near white-topped mountains or in cold climates. Many snow and ice sports are done indoors on artificial slopes and ice rinks in countries with even the warmest weather. Snow-making machines typically produce snow by forcing water and pressurized air through a snow cannon. In an artificial ice rink, a layer of water is frozen into ice on top of a slab of concrete containing pipes, which carry a chilled fluid.

GIRL TALK

In the 1960s, women who tried to join men's hockey teams were rejected. However, more and more women started to play anyway and to demand the opportunity to play at colleges and universities. The first Women's World Ice Hockey Championship took place in 1990, and in 1998, women's hockey became an Olympic sport.

BODY BENEFITS

There is no doubt about it, zooming around on the ice or snow, whether indoors or outside, is a great way to exercise. For example, ice-skating gets you fit and improves your balance and coordination. When ice-skating, participants strengthen and tone large muscles in their legs, buttocks, and core as they work hard to move across the ice. They also use and strengthen a lot of smaller muscles around their hips, knees, and ankles that do not normally get a workout.

Today there are more female hockey teams than ever. There are mixed-gender teams, too.

Smashing the Slopes

Girls and women have been smashing the slopes for years. Whether they are skiing in downhill races or chasing each other in a slalom race down a winding course, they are showing that they can hold their own in the world of skiing.

SKI RACES

Anyone interested in racing on skis has a choice of two types of skiing: Nordic and alpine. In Nordic ski races, athletes ski and jump over a cross-country race course of various distances, from 0.6-mile (1 km) sprints to 31-mile (50 km) races over hilly terrain. In alpine speed events, contestants do single runs down long, steep, fast courses featuring a few widely spaced turns and gates. Skiers are timed, and the fastest one through the course wins. In some contests, skiers have two races or chances, but in others, they get only one.

Alpine ski races are typically high-speed chases down steep snowy slopes.

SLALOM

Slalom racing is a kind of alpine downhill ski race. In slalom races, the poles, or gates, are placed closer together than in a standard ski race. Athletes have to zigzag back and forth, left and right, as they speed down the slopes. It not only hurts when they knock into the gates, but it also slows them down and reduces their chances of winning a race.

Giant slalom is longer distance and has faster, wider turns than ordinary slalom. Super giant slalom, or super-G, combines elements of downhill and giant slalom. It is a high-speed event, with wider turns than giant slalom.

It takes time and dedication to learn the skills needed for slalom skiing.

GIRL TALK

In slalom, skiers do not go around the gates: they ski through them! Spectators can hear the skier hitting the gate as they pass. In order to pass the gates without being slowed down, a skier must make sure their skis go through the gate rather than around it and that they do not get one ski hooked around the wrong side of the gate. Skiers also ensure their body remains in line and that they keep focused on where they are going.

To try snow and ice sports, indoor lessons are a great way to get started and are much cheaper than flying to the mountains if there are not any nearby. Lessons will not only teach the skills needed, but they will also help avoid injury. Anyone taking to the slopes should invest in the correct safety equipment—a helmet is vital for most skating, skiing, and snowboarding sessions.

Slalom is one of the most challenging events in skiing but it is exhilarating to compete in. To win a slalom event, athletes need speed, strong turns, great rhythm, and a lot of confidence. The key to slalom success is taking smooth, flowing, round turns through the slalom gates, not sharp, fast turns.

Mikaela Shiffrin shows the skills and technique that make her one of the best slalom skiers in the world.

Case Study

MIKAELA SHIFFRIN—AN UNSTOPPABLE FORCE!

Mikaela Shiffrin has the potential to be among the greatest skiers of all time. Her credentials include being a two-time Olympic gold medalist and World Cup alpine skier, the Overall World Cup champion twice, world champion in slalom three times, and a five-time winner of the World Cup discipline title in that event.

Mikaela holds her medal at the women's alpine slalom ceremony at the 2014 Olympics.

A NATURAL TALENT

Mikaela was born in Vale, Colorado, on March 13, 1995, and just two years later, her parents put her on skis. They soon spotted her talent. By the age of seven, she was already trailing her father, anesthesiologist Jeff Shiffrin, and telling him to go faster! Her mother, Eileen Shiffrin, a former nurse, helped Mikaela with her technique and even bought her a unicycle to help with her coordination and balance skills.

Mikaela went to high school at Burke Mountain Academy in Vermont, a school for talented ski racers located by a mountain. She trained hard and focused on her sport, a dedication that paid off when she was asked to join the World Cup tour in 2011 at age 16. Her mother, also her coach, traveled with her and is still at her side today—it is obviously a partnership that works.

At the 2014 Olympics in Sochi, Russia, Mikaela became the youngest slalom gold medalist ever.

Mikaela may be young, but she is so good at going fast that she makes slalom look easy.

Chapter 2

Ski Jumping

Ski jumping is an exciting and dynamic sport. It showcases the changes that are happening in the world of snow and ice sports. When most people imagine an athlete on a ski jump, they usually picture a man and not a woman, and that is no surprise. Until fairly recently, female skiers were not allowed to compete in ski jumping events because it was thought that women's bodies could not handle the sport.

It takes a lot of guts to take off into the air from the end of a terrifyingly high ski jump, like this!

COMPETITIONS

In ski jumping competitions, contestants ski down a steep ramp that curves upward at the end. They leap from the end, known as the takeoff point, and try to land as far as possible down the hill below. Most international competitions, including the Olympic Games, have ramps of 394 and 295 feet (120 and 90 m) high, known as the large hill and the normal hill respectively. Competitors get to make two jumps. The winner is the athlete who achieves the longest jump from the ramp on one of their two chances. The competitor's style and other factors also affect their final score.

V-SHAPED JUMPS

A ski jumper begins their jump from the top of the ramp on a scaffold or tower. They start off by skiing down the slope in a crouched position, in order to reduce air resistance and build up speed, until they reach the point of takeoff. At the takeoff point, they spring outward and upward. In the air, they use their body position to maximize their jump. Most ski jumpers use the V style. They point the tips of their skis outward in opposite directions to create a V shape, giving them the lift they need to stay longer in the air.

GIRL TALK

Men's ski jumping has been part of the Olympics since the first Winter Games, in Chamonix, France, in 1924. When female athletes were refused entry to the 2010 Olympic ski jump events, they were so angry that they sued the International Olympic Committee (IOC) for gender discrimination. This led to the IOC announcing in 2011 that a women's ski jumping event would be added to the 2014 Games in Sochi.

In ski jumping, athletes ski down a ramp at about 60 miles per hour (97 km/h) and typically fly farther than the length of a football field off the end of it.

It takes nerves of steel to become a ski jumper. Even though athletes learn on smaller slopes, at some point, they are going to have to climb high above the ground and face a long, curved slope, designed to eject them up into the air with nothing but their skis and skills to help them land safely again.

LEARNING TO SKI JUMP

Anyone interested in ski jumping should be able to take ski jumping lessons at their nearest dry ski slope, a snow dome, or while on a ski vacation. Learners often start out in the gym. They learn the correct positioning of their ankles, knees, back, and hips, and how their legs should start the process of a jump. The first jumps people try are so small that they are called ski bumps, not jumps. The bumps give participants the chance to practice building up speed down a slope and then springing up on their knees and leaning forward to take off. When they are confident in their technique, they can start with real, but small, ski jumps, of around 33 feet (10 m).

Ski jumping is probably the riskiest winter sport, but participants gain confidence as they learn the techniques they need to jump as safely as possible.

It is a long way down! This is the view that ski jumpers see from the very top of an Olympic-size ski jump.

GIRL TALK

Beginner ski jumps are not that big. While Olympic jumps measure 394 and 295 feet (120 and 90 m), beginner ski jumps are only 32, 60, or 65 feet (10, 18, or 20 m). But when athletes stand at the top of any jump for the first time, they are bound to feel the fear. If they can make that first jump, they may become hooked on this daring and exciting winter sport.

COOL KIT

The equipment needed for ski jumping is much the same as that of downhill skiing: boots, skis, poles, a ski jacket, and pants. Skiers must also wear a helmet. The skis used for ski jumping are typically longer and wider than normal skis, which helps ski jumpers stay in the air longer. Those who become really good at the sport may want to invest in a skintight ski jump bodysuit like Olympic skiers wear. These help to reduce air resistance.

As with most snow sports, ski jumpers wear snow goggles to protect their eyes, plus a helmet.

To become a champion ski jumper takes true grit. At the Olympics, athletes' jumps will be scrutinized by no fewer than five judges. A jump to what is known as the K-point (where the distance from the starting point equals the height of the hill) earns a ski jumper 60 points, and jumpers are awarded extra points for each 3 feet (1 m) that they travel beyond the K-point. A perfect ski jump earns 20 style points from each judge. Style points are taken off for errors such as touching the ground with a hand after landing or not landing with one foot before the other.

Being prepared in mind and body is important before a jump. Here, with the help of her coach, Sarah Hendrickson warms up before competing.

GIRL TALK

In the air, as well as making a V-shape with their legs, ski jumpers hold their arms slightly away from their body in order to maximize their surface area. This helps them "fly" for longer. Ski jumpers land with one foot ahead of the other and their arms spread to the side, with slightly bent knees, to absorb the impact as they touch down.

Case Study

SARAH HENDRICKSON—SKI JUMP STAR

In 2014, Sarah Hendrickson made history when she became the first woman ever to take part in a ski jumping competition in an Olympic Games, in Sochi, Russia.

Sarah has been skiing for as long as she could remember. She was born on August 1, 1994, in Salt Lake City, Utah, and spent weekends skiing all day every day with her family. She enjoyed skiing but loved the chance to jump off the bumps she met along the way even more. She was only five when her brother, who is three years older than her, took up ski jumping. Seeing him, she realized ski jumping was the sport for her and, by the age of seven, she was taking lessons.

One of Sarah's longest jumps is a staggering 469 feet (143 m), which she achieved at Lillehammer, Norway.

RECORD-BREAKING STAR

By 19, Sarah was a record breaker. She was the first American (male or female) to win a medal at a Junior World Championships. She became the World Cup Champion in 2012 and, in 2013, she became the second American to win a World Championship. In spite of battles with a painful knee injury, she managed to join Team USA for the 2014 and 2018 Olympic Games.

Chapter 3
Snowboarding

Die-hard snowboarders like nothing better than the adrenaline rush they get when racing on or jumping off the snow and doing tricks on their boards. Snowboarders can build up terrific speeds as they race downhill, and it takes real courage and skill to snowboard off a slope and perform tricks and flips in midair. Snowboarding is also amazingly entertaining for spectators.

Today, more and more women are heading for the slopes to enjoy the exhilarating and challenging sport of snowboarding.

THE SECRETS OF SNOWBOARDING

Snowboarders stand on a single board, which is attached to their boots by mounted bindings. Unlike skiing, in which athletes face forward, riders position their feet roughly perpendicular to the board and its direction. Snowboarding was inspired by skateboarding, skiing, sledding, and surfing, and was developed in the United States in the 1960s and 1970s. It became a Winter Olympic sport in 1998.

PIPE DREAMS

There are different types of snowboarding. In the 2018 Winter Olympics, there were five snowboarding events:

- Big air: Competitors ride a snowboard down a slope then perform tricks after launching off very large jumps.

- Halfpipe: Competitors perform tricks while going from one side of a semicircular pipe to the other.

- Parallel giant slalom: Two competitors compete in two parallel slalom courses in which they must weave around offset poles, or gates, as fast as they can.

- Slopestyle: Snowboarders perform a variety of acrobatic moves while speeding down a sloping course, which has rails for sliding and ramps for jumping.

- Snowboard cross: Riders race against each other down a course with jumps, berms (or banks), and other obstacles.

Halfpipes are not just for boys! This supergirl gets some air on a halfpipe.

WHAT A WORKOUT!

Snowboarding is a high-intensity aerobic workout and is great for building up core strength as well as working leg muscles. It also improves balance. And, if done outside, there is the added benefit of getting a lot of fresh air, which makes people feel good.

GIRL TALK

Big air events are only for the bold. The long, steep ramp to the large kicker jump is 160 feet (49 m) high. This launches snowboarders spinning through the air as they perform their big, daring tricks.

In big air events, athletes are judged on the technical difficulty of their tricks, the size of the jump, and their style and landing.

Shredding the Slopes

Snowboarding might sound difficult, but riders can pick up the basics very quickly. Anyone who thinks they might like to try snowboarding should give it a try. They can take lessons in an indoor ski center, most of which are lined with actual snow for that real snowboarding experience.

Knowing how to maintain a balanced position on the board is an important skill for beginners to learn.

LEARNING THE ROPES

The first things to learn are the basics. To go fast down a slope, the rider points their snowboard straight down, or forward. To control the speed of the snowboard, they need to position it horizontally across the slope, tilting forward or backward with their toes or heels. Then they learn to make S-shaped turns down the slope. The first few attempts are best done with the help of a coach, who will hold the rider's hands and guide them as they gradually gain confidence.

NEW TRICKS AND SKILLS

When a rider has mastered the basics, so they can stop, control their speed, and make various turns on their snowboard, they can start to learn tricks and more advanced skills. To start with, most people learn some tricks on the flat, such as popping, which is jumping by sinking down through the knees and pushing off the ground with both feet. Gradually they can add new tricks and higher jumps to their repertoire. Most people train to do more ambitious tricks at an indoor facility with trampolines and foam mats, where they can be more daring without risking injuries.

A snowboard looks like a large, nonwheeled skateboard, to which the rider's feet are attached with bindings.

GEAR UP

Before riders hit the slopes with their snowboards, they should make sure that they have the right equipment and that it fits them correctly. Boots and bindings must be the right size for their feet and all riders must wear a helmet. Goggles will protect their eyes from bright sunlight and objects like tree branches that could hit them in the eye. Snowboarders also wear knee and elbow pads. Beginners may also wear padded pants to cushion their falls.

GIRL TALK

Snowboarding can be a little like learning to ride a bicycle on the road. Riders have to learn to share the road or trail with others, so they have to watch out for other people to avoid crashing into them, risking injury to themselves and others.

Ski slopes can be busy, so riders need to be aware of other skiiers at all times.

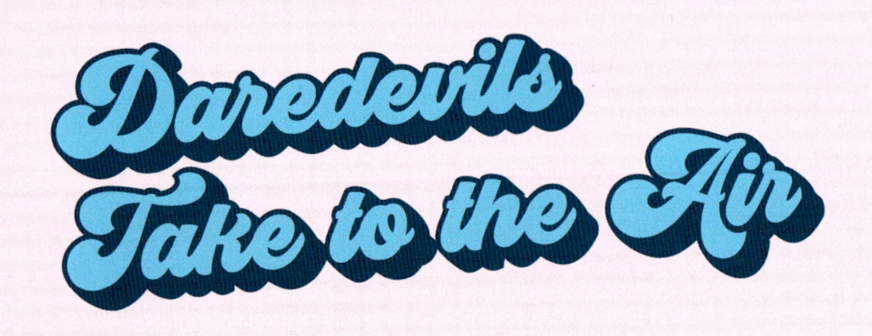

Daredevils Take to the Air

Female daredevil snowboarders can enjoy their sport in different ways. Some focus on freeriding: riding for fun up and down mountain slopes, often riding massive peaks. Others enjoy freestyle snowboarding for pleasure or to compete in freestyle competitions around the world, which often showcase ramps and walls that are entirely made of snow or ice. Getting really good at the sport takes time and effort, but the thrill of achieving a high jump or a great trick will make all that well worth it!

US champion Chloe Kim competes in the women's halfpipe final at the Olympics in South Korea.

GIRL TALK

Many athletes have little rituals or superstitions about things they do before an event to bring them luck. Olympic rider Chloe Kim knocks twice on her snowboard before starting a run. Snowboards are made from wood so she knocks on wood for good luck—and it has certainly worked out well for her so far!

Case Study

CHLOE KIM—GOLD STAR

When Chloe Kim won the women's halfpipe gold medal at the 2018 Pyeongchang Winter Olympics in South Korea, she had two reasons to celebrate. She had beaten her competitors to take the top award in her sport and she had done so in Korea, in front of family who still live in her parents' native country.

Chloe celebrates her victory at the 2018 Olympics. She hopes to do it all again at the 2022 Games.

FEARLESS AND FIERCE

When you see her face on magazine covers or on television, Chloe is all smiles, but during contests, she is a fierce competitor who has worked very hard to get to the top of her game.

Chloe was born April 23, 2000, in Long Beach, California. Her father started teaching her to snowboard when she was just four years old. She was such a natural that she started competing when she was six years old. From 8 to 10 years old, she trained in Switzerland, before returning to California.

By 2013, Chloe was a member of the US snowboarding team. Although she was good enough to ride in the 2014 Olympics, she was too young to compete. So, she trained all out to prepare for the 2018 Games. By then, there was a lot of expectation for her to succeed. Some thought she might crack under the pressure, but Chloe totally crushed it and has the gold medal to prove it.

Chloe shows the incredible style and skills that earned her that gold medal in South Korea in 2018.

Chapter 4 Speed Skating

Speed skating is a fast-paced sport in which competitors move at high speeds around an oval track made of ice. In some races, skaters compete directly against each other, adding an element of danger to the races, as they risk crashing into each other and ending up rolling onto the ice.

Speed skaters love to go fast! They can reach speeds of up to 40 miles per hour (64 km/h).

ICE RACES

Speed skating was originally used as a rapid form of transportation across frozen canals in the Netherlands. It was so popular there that it became the national sport by the middle of the nineteenth century. Speed skating gradually spread to other countries and, in 1924, it appeared at the first Winter Olympics in Chamonix. Today, races can take place on indoor or outdoor rinks.

TYPES OF SPEED SKATING

In the Olympic Games there are two types of speed-skating race: long-track and short-track. Long-track events are timed. Typically, two skaters compete at a time, in separate lanes. Whoever posts the fastest time wins. There is also a long-track team pursuit event. In this event, groups of three athletes skate the distance together. In short-track speed skating, athletes compete against each other rather than against the clock. Several skaters line up next to each other, battling for position throughout the race. It does not matter how fast they go: the winner is simply the first skater to cross the finish line.

Long-track speed skating is all about competing against yourself to achieve the fastest time.

Short-track skaters usually race at top speeds of around 35 miles per hour (56 km/h).

GIRL TALK

Speed skating is a great aerobic workout. It builds muscle strength and stamina. Speed skating also improves balance and coordination as skaters have to be able to keep their balance on very thin blades while moving in a precise way.

Fast and Furious

Speed skating appeals to daredevils who enjoy the thrill of speeding down a long lane of ice with the wind whipping their face and hair, all the while on a pair of ice skates. Learning to speed skate takes determination, skill, and bravery.

STAY SAFE

Skaters can take lessons on an indoor ice rink or skate outdoors on frozen ponds and lakes. However, skaters should skate outdoors only in places that are approved for skating and always accompanied by an adult. Skaters should never risk skating on ice that has not been approved, because even though an area of ice might look thick and strong, it may not hold the skaters' weight.

GIRL TALK

When speed skaters have built up speed, they tuck one arm behind their back. This makes them more aerodynamic. If they have their arms out, they are creating more air resistance and will slow down.

Skaters cross their outer skate over their inner skate, and swing the outside arm, to accelerate around bends.

LEARNING TO SKATE

The first thing skaters learn to do (after standing up on their ice skates) is put one foot down, push, shift their weight, and pick up the other foot. Their toe, knee, and face on one side should all be aligned with their opposite arm and leg. Countering that weight is their hip, so they have to stick out their hip to stay stable. All ice skate blades have two edges, like two parallel knives. When they move forward, skaters should rest on both edges of the blade. To lean into a turn, they rest on just one edge or the other. At a sharp turn, speed skaters do crossovers. They cross their outer foot in front of the inner, so just the inside edge of the outer skate and the outside edge of the inner skate touches the ice.

Speed skates have longer, thinner, and straighter blades than figure or hockey skates. They also have very low ankles, so skaters can bend their knees and get their body weight closer to the ice to help them move faster.

SAFE SKATES

Anyone who takes up speed skating should purchase their own set of ice skates, rather than borrowing or renting them. This is because their feet need to be fitted properly. To reduce the risk of hurting their ankles, skaters should always lace their skates firmly and check that, when they stand up, their heel is at the back of the boot and their toe does not touch the front.

Speed skating is such a fast and furious sport that, at first, only men were allowed to enter competitions. It was not until the 1960 Winter Olympics in Squaw Valley, California, that women's speed skating was officially included in the Olympic program. Today, women's speed skating events attract crowds of enthusiastic supporters, ready to be entertained by these awesome athletes.

ON TRACK TO WIN

International speed skating events take place on a track or course that has straight sides and ends curved in such a way that the skaters do not need to slow down to take them. In races with two competitors on a two-lane track, the athletes take turns to skate on the slightly shorter inner curve. A space, called the crossing line, is left open along the back stretch for the skaters to switch tracks.

GIRL TALK

Some speed skating races are won by a thousandth of a second, so athletes do what they can to reduce air resistance. To minimize drag, skaters hunch right over, keeping their backs flat like a table top. They also wear one-piece, skintight suits, often with hoods, which make the racers as streamlined as possible.

Skaters do all they can to increase their speed and to shave fractions of a second off their time.

Case Study

MAAME BINEY—SHORT-TRACK SPEED SKATING STAR

In 2018, Maame Biney earned her place in the history books when she became the first African American female speed skater to qualify for the Olympics, an achievement she described as "crazy awesome." Not only that, but Maame was also one of the youngest members of Team USA who headed to South Korea for the Winter Olympics that year.

FIGURING IT OUT

Maame's skating career could have turned out very differently. Born in Ghana, West Africa, on January 28, 2000, Maame moved to the United States to live with her father. By six years old she was taking figure skating lessons. When she was told she skated too fast, Maame took it as a compliment and switched to speed skating.

Since then, there has been no looking back. Maame was delighted when she made the US team for the 2018 Olympics, but knew she did not stand a chance of a medal there. Now she has her sights set on the 2022 Olympics in China, where she plans to blow away the world in the short-track speed skating event.

The Winter Olympics are the highlight of any snow and ice sportswoman's career. Being part of Team USA and participating is an incredible experience.

Chapter 5
Ice Climbing

For many ice climbers, it is the element of danger that makes them so passionate about their sport. Climbing up the side of a high wall of ice, with the risk of falling at any moment, is not everyone's idea of a good time, but many of those who try ice climbing become hooked on the thrills and challenges it gives them.

Scaling a wall of ice, with a slick, treacherous surface, can be very dangerous.

CLIMBING THE ICE

Ice climbing developed from rock and mountain climbing. High up on mountains, where areas of snow and ice form, climbers had to get past these slippery and challenging obstacles to proceed up a slope. To do so, climbers began to develop specialized tools and equipment. Over time, some climbers began to enjoy climbing the ice so much that they chose to do specific ice climbing trips instead of rock climbing.

HOW IS IT DONE?

On a vertical ice climb, climbers use a tool called an ice ax. The sharp end of the ice ax is a pick, used for hooking and swinging into the ice. They can then use this as a grip to help them pull themselves up with their legs. Next they use ice screws and ropes as a safety measure to protect themselves from falling. They use the ice pick to hack a hole to insert ice screws into the ice, then attach a rope. The rope is clipped to a safety harness worn around their body.

TYPES OF ICE

Ice climbers tackle two different types of ice: alpine ice and water ice. Alpine ice is the ice you find higher up a mountain. This ice usually started out as snow that settled on the slopes. Over a long period of time, layers of snow turned into hard-packed ice, sometimes called blue ice. Water ice is usually found at the side of a glacier or frozen waterfall. Water ice is a frozen flow of water, such as a waterfall. It may melt then freeze again, so it often has large bumps, ridges, and icicles.

GIRL TALK

Ice climbers have to constantly watch the ice as they climb. Ice screws are only as strong as the ice into which they have been screwed. Climbers must try to find blue-tinted ice or ice that is stained yellow from minerals because these will hold their ice screws well. Pure white ice is usually full of air and may not support the screws.

A rope and harness keep an ice climber from falling too far if they slip.

Get a Grip!

Hacking up tall walls of ice and gripping onto the ice with fingertips can be exhilarating, but beginners should start indoors before attempting a mountain face. Indoor ice climbing walls are a great and safe way to learn to ice climb or work on improving skills. They have simple routes for beginners that have easy, angled snow slopes, as well as more challenging walls.

Crampon spikes stick out from climbing shoes so wearers can stab them into the ice for extra grip.

GEAR UP

As well as warm clothing, a helmet is a vital piece of equipment that will protect the climber's head and eyes from falls and also from falling chunks of ice. As well as an ice ax for hacking into the ice, climbers also need crampons. Crampons are metal claws that come attached to the bottom of climbing boots or can be clipped onto boots. Climbers kick the sharp fangs of the crampons into the ice as they climb to help them grip onto steep walls of slippery ice.

PRACTICE MAKES PERFECT

At an indoor ice wall, beginners can learn ice climbing basics such as how to swing the ice ax. To do this, they must keep their elbow high and lined up with their hand and the tool. The straighter they can swing, the more precise a hit they will make in the ice. If the pick does not go into the ice well, climbers must remove it and try again. They then practice stepping up with both feet before swinging the pick again at a slightly higher level and moving both feet slightly higher up. Beginners may need to kick their crampons into the ice a few times to get a good, solid grip.

GOING DOWN

What goes up must come down! After making it to the top, ice climbers have to be able to climb or lower themselves down again safely. Some athletes make their way down by climbing, too. Abseiling, or rappelling, is when climbers use a rope fixed to a higher point to descend. When people learn to abseil, they learn to control how quickly and carefully they descend.

GIRL TALK

For safety, ice climbers usually work with at least one other climber and they also carry an avalanche beacon. An avalanche is when a mass of snow, ice, or rocks falls rapidly down a mountainside. Avalanches can happen suddenly, so climbers can use their beacons to send out signals, which help rescuers find people buried or trapped by avalanches.

Climbers must time a climb, so they do not have to come down a dangerous ice wall in the dark.

Ice climbing can be a very challenging and dangerous activity, so it is perhaps no surprise that it was a sport enjoyed only by men for many years. Then, girls and women got the ice-climbing bug and it is estimated that the number of female climbers has grown by more than 50 percent in the last 10 years.

Climbing outdoors is exhilarating but also potentially more dangerous than indoor ice climbing.

GOING FOR GOLD

Some female ice climbers do the activity just for fun, for exercise, or as a way of enjoying being outdoors. Others take it more seriously and train for the Ice Climbing World Cup. In the World Cup, athletes compete in speed-climbing events, which are like vertical sprints on ice. Until now, ice climbing has not been part of the official Winter Olympic program, but the International Climbing and Mountaineering Federation (UIAA) is striving for ice-climbing competitions to be included in the Winter Olympics in Beijing in 2022.

GIRL TALK

Outdoor walls of ice provide a unique challenge for climbers. The ice outdoors is always changing. It melts, gets thicker, or the wind blows the water in a different way as it freezes. This means an outdoor ice climb is never the same from one day to the next. This makes it more challenging and exciting, but also more dangerous because climbers cannot predict what the climb will be like.

Case Study

KENDRA STRITCH— THE SPIRIT OF ADVENTURE

US ice climber Kendra Stritch's motto is "Always have fun and adventure." Kendra had been both a rugby player and a slalom ski racer before she began learning to ice climb and competing in international ice climbing competitions. Her competitive spirit and hunger for a challenge soon won her a gold medal at the 2015 Ice Climbing World Cup, the sport's top competition.

Kendra loves the thrill of scaling walls of frozen water. It's no secret that she is on the way to the top of her challenging sport!

When Kendra first tried ice climbing with her brother, a champion climber himself, she thought it was boring because she was just trying to climb straight up the ice. But when she tackled a more difficult, textured wall of ice, on which she had to use different techniques and body positioning, she was hooked.

Kendra honed her skills on the frozen waterfalls and high icy cliffs of Minnesota, before traveling the world to take part in competitions. Kendra loves the challenge of competition speed climbing, in which climbers have to sprint up a vertical 50-foot (15 m) wall. She has earned the North American speed champion title in ice climbing three years running.

Chapter 6

Luge and Skeleton Racing

It takes a certain kind of confidence and courage to take part in luge and skeleton contests. In these extreme sports, athletes ride a sled at high speeds down an ice-covered course with steep, banking turns. These are among the most exciting sports in the Olympic Games and they require a high level of bravery and skill.

Luge racers zoom down the track on their back with their feet first.

ULTIMATE SLEDDING

The luge is often called ultimate sledding. In luge competitions, racers with feet stretched out in front of them slide down an icy track with only a helmet for protection. The racer starts off sitting on a flat sled. Then, they pull themselves forward to begin the run, lying down and only lifting their head just enough to see where they are going. The racer angles their body to steer down the course on the sled, sometimes reaching speeds of up to 90 miles per hour (145 km/h). Races are so hard-fought that they can be won by margins as slight as two-thousandths of a second.

LOOKING AT THE LUGE

The word "luge" comes from the French word for sled, and the sport was developed in Switzerland. Luge racers ride a flat sled with bars on either side for them to hold onto as they lie down. The sled is made of molded fiberglass, with two metal runners, called steels, which curve upward. Luges generally weigh between 50 and 60 pounds (23 and 27 kg). There are no steering wheels or levers, so the only way a racer can alter the direction of the sled is by adjusting the angle of their body. Luge racers typically steer by pressing their legs against the runners.

The steels underneath a luge sled are narrow and sharp like ice skates.

GIRL TALK

One reason luge racers can race at such high speeds is aerodynamics. When an athlete lies on their back as they slide down the track, they have less surface area and create less air resistance. This helps them go faster.

Luge racers tackle the track's twists and turns using subtle body movements.

Loving the Luge

In both men's and women's singles luge races, the nail-biting competition takes two days, with every contestant doing two runs on each day. Each athlete's four times are added up, and the person with the fastest total time is declared the winner.

SAFETY GEAR

The risk of injury is fairly high so all competitors must wear a strong, rigid helmet and visor to keep their head safe when speeding down the track. They also wear a skintight rubber suit to reduce air resistance, and spiked gloves to help them hold themselves in position and speed off the starting line. They wear racing boots that help them keep their feet and legs locked in a straight position.

LEARNING TO LAUNCH A LUGE

At the start of the luge course, an athlete holds onto handles on each side of the luge and rocks back and forth to build momentum. Then, they propel themselves onto the course and paddle their gloved hands across the first 10 feet (3 m) or so of the track. This helps them build up some speed before they lie down on the sled and take off downhill.

GIRL TALK

Getting a good start is the most important way of ensuring a fast speed in a luge race and it requires a very strong upper body and arms. That is why luge athletes train hard to build upper-body muscles through exercises such as swimming and weight lifting.

If a racer makes a good start, all that is left to do is steer the course.

Case Study

EMILY SWEENEY—JOIN THE SWEEN TEAM

When watching her race, Emily Sweeney's friends and family show their support by wearing caps with "Sween Team" written on them. The Sween Team was in full voice when Emily proudly won her first World Cup gold medal in 2017. After that she set her sights on an Olympic medal, but this challenge proved to be a more difficult and dangerous one. When Emily raced at the 2018 Winter Olympics she was full of confidence but, unfortunately, she crashed on her final run, catastrophically losing control as she entered a corner. Thankfully, she escaped without any serious injuries and lived on to race another day.

Emily is a member of the Army National Guard and enjoys playing lacrosse to keep her fit and strong for luge.

The Skeleton

Just as its name suggests, skeleton is a scary type of sport. Skeleton riders race fast downhill on a flat sled similar to the luge. The difference between this sport and luge racing is that skeleton athletes hurtle down the icy track while lying face down on their stomach, facing forward, head first. Competitors remain aerodynamic by keep their face barely 1 inch (2.5 cm) from the ice as they speed down tracks at up to 90 miles per hour (140 km/h).

Skeleton riders face the track ahead of them as they hurtle down it at high speed.

THE SKELETON

Like a luge, there are neither brakes nor a steering mechanism on a skeleton sled. However, the skeleton sled is heavier and thinner than a luge. For women, the maximum weight of sled and driver, including equipment, is 203 pounds (92 kg). The maximum height and length of a sled is between 31 and 47 inches (80 and 120 cm) long, and between 3 and 8 inches (8 and 20 cm) high. Skeleton sleds are made of steel. They have runners on the bottom that run along the ice and are bowed to decrease the total area that touches the ice. Skeleton sleds also have bumpers that reduce the impact on the sled and the athlete if they hit the walls of the track.

RIDING THE SKELETON

To stand any chance of winning a skeleton race, athletes must make a fast start. A skeleton racer does not start out in the sled. They have to push their sled and run as fast as they can for about 100 feet (30 m) before jumping face first onto the moving sled, with their feet and head hanging over the ends. Then, riders use small movements of their body, head, and shoulders to control and steer the sled down the course. Sometimes they reach out and tap a toe on the ice in the direction they want to turn.

It takes a lot of skill to get an ice sled started on a skeleton run and then jump onto it while it is moving.

GIRL TALK

There is some confusion about how the skeleton got its name. Some people think it is because of the skeleton-like shape of early sleds. Others believe that it came from people trying to pronounce "kjaelke," which is the Norwegian word for "ice sled."

Skeleton Girls

To win skeleton races, athletes need lightning-fast reflexes to ensure they take turns and corners at high speeds. Before a race, athletes take trial runs down the track to learn every corner and get to know the perfect line along the course.

WHAT EVERY ATHLETE NEEDS TO COMPETE

- Race suits are made from lightweight and tight-fitting fabric called Lycra, to help make the riders aerodynamic and to maximize their speed.

- Skeleton helmets are usually made of fiberglass, which is strong enough to protect an athlete's skull in case they crash, but also light enough that they can hold up their heads. Helmets cover the face and the chin and have clear Perspex visors.

- Shoes have 300 needlelike spikes on the soles that look like a brush or broom. These spikes grip the ice at the start of the race so that athletes can push their sled quickly.

As long as riders wear the correct gear and do not take unnecessary risks, they should be safe while competing.

GIRL TALK

Skeleton was removed from Olympic competitions after 1948 because the Olympic committee deemed it too dangerous for riders to go downhill headfirst. The women's event was added when skeleton was reintroduced to the Olympic program in 2002.

Case Study

KATIE UHLAENDER—AN AMERICAN EAGLE

When Katie Uhlaender competes in the skeleton, she tucks her hair into a helmet emblazoned with the American Eagle. Katie has won the women's Skeleton World Cup title twice and has competed in a total of four Winter Olympics.

Katie was born on July 17, 1984, in Vail, Colorado, and grew up in McGregor, Texas. It was her father Ted, once an outfielder for the Cincinnati Reds baseball team, who inspired her love of sport. Katie played baseball, softball, and golf, and took part in skiing and powerlifting before she tried the skeleton. Since her dad passed away in 2009, she has worn his 1972 National League Championship Series (NLCS) ring in his memory.

Katie's dedication and determination are an inspiration to other female skeleton athletes around the world.

Katie took part in her first skeleton competition in 2004. She trains so hard that she has even been able to compete in weightlifting events. Her advice to beginners who are interested in the sport is to watch other athletes closely and to make sure they understand every aspect of what they are doing and why they are doing it.

Becoming a Supergirl

In the past, girls and women may have been put off by the macho atmosphere that surrounded snow and ice sports, but today, these fun activities are open to everyone. There are more and more girls and women flocking to the mountains, artificial ski slopes, and rinks to try out a new challenge.

GIRL POWER

Becoming a supergirl does not mean you have to train to be a medal-winning snow and ice athlete. Learning snowboarding, speed skating, ice climbing, or any of these unusual and sometimes extreme sports will give you confidence, strength, fitness, and a determination to succeed in all walks of life, and those are the characteristics that make a true supergirl. Many supergirls will simply enjoy doing snow and ice sports as a hobby or a regular workout, and appreciate the chance to make new friends.

GIVE IT A GO!

Although many athletes at the top of their game started training and competing at a young age, this should not keep you from trying a new snow and ice sport. If you do try and you think you could be good enough to enter competitions, you must be prepared to put in many hours of practice, sometimes at indoor snow or ice centers far from home, so it will not be easy. But, if you really have the dedication and determination to succeed, why not give it a go?

Women from all over the world are starting to compete in and win ice and snow sports at the highest level.

There are many careers to choose from, giving women a chance to earn a living from the snow and ice sports that they love.

SNOW AND ICE CAREERS

As well as taking part in snow and ice sports for fun or to compete at a high level, some people make a different kind of career in their chosen field. Some snow and ice supergirls become coaches, teaching other people to ski, snowboard, and speed skate. Others get jobs organizing events, such as championships and games, or promoting competitions to ensure plenty of people come to watch them. Others become sports journalists, writing reports about ice and snow sports events and stars.

GIRL TALK

No matter which snow or ice sport you choose, put safety first. Wear the right equipment, learn the correct techniques, and if you are outdoors, do not forget to wear layers of warm clothes and plenty of sunscreen. Sunlight reflects off the snow and ice, burning skin quickly.

Sunshine reflects off snow, so large goggles like these are important when enjoying your chosen sport on the snow.

Find out just how great girls can be at all kinds of sports—then find your inner supergirl and try them out for yourself! There are a variety of ice and snow sports, so there is sure to be one that appeals to you.

Regardless of what sport you want to try, whether it is speed skating, ski jumping, or snowboarding, there are clubs and gyms around the United States where you can learn some new skills.

SLALOM

If you want to learn to slalom ski, you need to find a club and a coach. For advice, contacts, and more, go to this website, where you can home in on your chosen field:
http://my.ussa.org/global/getting-started

SKI JUMPING

If you want to learn to ski jump, log on to this website to find out more about the sport:
www.skijumpingusa.com

SNOWBOARDING

To find a club and a coach to learn snowboarding skills, as well as advice and contacts, go to this website:
https://usskiandsnowboard.org/search?keys=snowboarding

SPEED SKATING

If you think speed skating might be the sport for you, this website could help. You can search for programs near you and download a speed skating curriculum:
www.learntoskateusa.com/speed-skating-lessons

ICE CLIMBING

To locate an indoor climbing gym where you can learn to rock and ice climb, type your location into this page:
www.indoorclimbing.com/worldgyms.html

LUGE RACING

Register at this site if you would like to join the United States Luge Association:
www.teamusa.org/usa-luge/slider-search

SKELETON RACING

To find out more about trying skeleton racing, go to:
www.teamusa.org/USA-bobsled-skeleton-federation/about-us/about-the-sports

Slalom may look difficult, but with the right coaching, you, too, could take to the slopes.

TOP TIP

Whether you have booked some coaching sessions or not, online tutorials are really helpful when processing the visual "how to" around a new snow and ice sport technique or trick. There are many to be found on social media platforms such as YouTube.

absorb soak up

adrenaline a substance released in the body when people feel a strong emotion, such as excitement, fear, or anger. Adrenaline causes the heart to beat faster and gives the person more energy.

aerobic describes an exercise that makes people breathe hard and the blood pump faster through their veins as it carries oxygen to the muscles

aerodynamic describes a shape that is designed to move through the air quickly

air resistance the force air exerts against a moving object, slowing it down

anesthesiologist a doctor who specializes in giving anesthetics to patients to prevent their feeling pain during surgery

artificial made by people, not by nature

coordination the ability to use different parts of the body together smoothly and efficiently

core the muscles within the torso

discrimination treating a person unfairly because of who they are or because they possess certain characteristics

drag the force air exerts against a moving object, slowing it down

gender the state of being male or female

impact the force or action of one object hitting another

lift the force that directly opposes the weight of an object and holds it in the air

parallel describes objects that are side by side and have the same distance continuously between them

perpendicular standing at right angles

Perspex a type of clear plastic

pressurized when air inside a container is packed more tightly, or has higher pressure, than the air outside it

runners the thin, strong, blade-like parts on which a sled or sleigh slides

snow cannon a machine that makes artificial snow and blows it onto ski slopes

stamina physical or mental strength that allows a person to continue doing something for a long time

streamlined a sleek shape that reduces air resistance, increasing speed and ease of movement

surface area the total area of the surface of a three-dimensional object

unicycle a cycle with a single wheel

vertical describes something standing or pointing straight up, or at an angle of 90 degrees to a horizontal surface

visor a movable part of a helmet that can be pulled down to cover the face

BOOKS

Garrison, Hal. *Ice Climbing* (Daredevil Sports). New York, NY: Gareth Stevens Publishing, 2018.

Katirgis, Jane, and Bob Woods. *Racing Snowmobiles* (Speed Racers). Berkeley Heights, NJ: Enslow Publishing, 2018.

Labrecque, Ellen. *Snowboarding* (21st Century Skills Library: Global Citizens: Olympic Sports). North Mankato, MN: Cherry Lake Publishing, 2018.

Shea, Therese. *Rock and Ice Climbing* (Sports to the Extreme). New York, NY: Rosen Central, 2015.

Whiting, Jim. *Snowboarding* (Odysseys in Extreme Sports). Mankato, MN: Creative Paperbacks, 2018.

WEBSITES

Learn how to keep safe if you try a new snow and ice sport at:
https://kidshealth.org/en/kids/winter-sports.html

Discover the science of sled racing at:
www.insidescience.org/news/engineering-ice-out-bobsled-luge-and-skeleton

Read more about Olympic speed skating at:
www.olympic.org/speed-skating

Get some tips on snowboarding at:
www.wikihow.com/snowboard

Index